THE SPIRIT OF
Liberation

By Bishop E. Bernard Jordan

ISBN 0-939241-09-9

The Spirit of Liberation

2nd Printing

DEDICATION

THE SPIRIT OF LIBERATION is dedicated to my son Yakim Manasseh Robert Jordan, an emerging prophetic born that will trumpet the message of liberation to the farthest corners of the earth defying man-made limitation. Fear not, the Spirit of the Liberator will guide and protect you as you proclaim liberty to the captives.

In Gratitude

We'd like to give the following individuals a special thank you for their faithfulness and support in helping to make our dream come true:

Josette Bassett
Margaret C. Bowling
Cecile Brown
Pastor David Brown &
    New Destiny Christian Center
Pastor Precious Davis
Pastor Richard Eberiga
Elder Fitzgerald A. King
Jacqueline Jeffries
Bessie Jones
Deborah Lloyd
Sandra Rodriguez
Yolanda Rojas
Dr. Gertrude Smith
Michelle Walker

Because of their generosity and obedience to the Spirit of God, we know that they have opened the door for miracles, and we believe that He shall cause the gems of wisdom that are contained within these pages to be made manifest in each of their lives, for the reward of the Lord is sure and addeth no sorrow!

In His Love and Service,
Bishop E. Bernard & Pastor Debra Jordan

TABLE OF CONTENTS

AUTHOR'S PREFACE

This book trumpets the Spirit of Liberation — God's plan for man to dominate the earth, not other men, and to be made free through the liberating gospel of Jesus Christ. It issues a clarion call for blacks to arise and take their rightful roles in society. And, it confronts racist attitudes in the Church and in society at large that have attempted to re-make man into an image of a nigger instead of the image of God.

It's tight but it's right!

Like its predecessor the Spirit of the Oppressor, I expect this book to arouse anger. I *know* it will be controversial. I anticipate that response! Why? Because as a Prophet of God I am commissioned to undress the lie that is rampant in our nation. Like Jeremiah I do not consider the faces of my opposition, but only speak what God tells me to speak. In this hour, he is speaking Liberation, Liberation, Liberation! He is uncovering the gross darkness of racism and oppression and bringing Truth. Truth is not a philosophy, but a Person. That Person is Jesus Christ.

Men have been waiting to hear Truth. But how can they hear without a preacher? There is a great need for prophetic voices to arise and proclaim the truth that makes men free, not the oppressive "pie-in-the sky" milk and cookies message that has historically emanated from the church. That message enslaved an entire nation of people and promulgated the lie that Christianity is a white man's religion. It is time for Truth to come forth. In these pages, I present Him to you in black and white!

Read it and weep. If you are among the oppressed, this

book will challenge you to walk upright with a new attitude and a new self-image. For you, "weeping may endure for a night, but joy comes in the morning."

But, for those of you who vigorously fight the liberation message: cry aloud and spare not. I pray that your tears will be those of repentance. I pray that you will repent — turn around — and embrace God. For you're not fighting a man or a message, you're actually fighting God. For where the Spirit of the Lord is there is Liberty. That's the word of God.

- Bishop E. Bernard Jordan

CHAPTER ONE
THE SPIRIT OF LIBERATION

Three hundred years ago, men of another race discovered a strong people, a people who possessed ingenuity, patience, skill and strength. This race of people were studied very carefully. Their family structure, honor and integrity were unequalled in the earth. Their physical and mental capacity for labor was unchallenged. They were a people marked with creativity of God, whom they wholeheartedly acknowledged as their Creator. They were a people who would soon be cruelly subjugated to the whims and demands of another race of people who would castrate their lifestyle and render their attempt to maintain their freedom impotent.

One individual, by the name of Willie Lynch, is famous for his formation of a demonic strategy that enslaved an entire nation of people. He wrote a significant speech in 1712 that contained keys of division, which are still in use today, to promote bondage and weaken the social structure of an entire race. These keys need to be identified, uprooted, and condemned by all of us. The following speech was the catalyst for the inveterate captivity of black people:

PROPHETIC PRINCIPLE # 1

Keys of division promoted bondage and weakened the African Race.

"Gentlemen, I greet you here on the banks of the James River in the year of our Lord. First, I shall thank you, the gentlemen of the colony of Virginia, for bringing me here. I am here to help you solve some of your problems with your slaves. Your invitation reached me on my modest plantation in the West Indies, where I have experimented with some of the newest and still oldest methods for maintaining control of slaves.

Ancient Rome would envy us if my program is implemented (which it was, B.J.). As our boats sail South on the James River, named for our illustrious king, whose version of the Bible we cherish. I saw enough to know that your problem is not unique.

While Rome used cords of wood as crosses for standing

human bodies along its old highways in great numbers. You are here using the tree and the rope on occasion. I caught the whiff of a dead slave hanging from a tree a couple of miles back. You are not only losing valuable stock by hanging, but you are having uprisings. Slaves are running away. Your crops are sometimes left in the field too long for maximum profit. You suffer occasional fires and your animals are killed. Gentlemen, you know what your problems are.

I do not need to elaborate, I am not here to eliminate your problem, I am here to introduce you to a method of solving them. In my bag here, I have a fool-proof method for controlling your black slaves. I guarantee everyone of you that if installed correctly, it will control the slaves for at least 300 years. My method is simple and the members of your family or anyone can use it.

I have outlined a number of differences among the slaves. And I take these differences and make them bigger. I use fear, distrust, and envy for control purposes. These methods have worked on my modest plantation in the West Indies. And it will work throughout the South.

Take this simple little list of differences and think about

PROPHETIC PRINCIPLE #2

Fear, distrust and envy equate to control.

them. On the top of my list is age, but it is there only because it starts with an A. The second is color, or shade. There is intelligence, size, sex, size of plantation, status on plantation, attitude of the owner, whether the slaves live in the valley on a hill, East, West, North, South, have fine or coarse hair, or is tall or short. Now that you have a list of differences, I shall give you an outline of action.

But before that, I shall assure you that distrust is stronger than trust and envy is stronger than adulation, respect or admiration.

The black slaves, after receiving this indoctrination, shall carry on and will become self refueling, self generating for hundreds of years, maybe thousands. Don't forget, you must pit the old black male versus the young black male and the young black male against the old black male. You must use the dark skinned slave versus the light skinned slave and the light skinned slave versus the dark skinned slave. You must also have your white servants and overseers distrust all blacks, but it is necessary for them to trust and depend on us. They must love, respect and trust only us.

Gentlemen, these kits are your control, use them, have your wives and children use them, never miss an opportunity. My plan is guaranteed and the good thing about this plan is that if used intensely for one year, the slaves themselves will remain perpetually distrustful.

Thank you gentlemen, Willie Lynch."

This is a letter that is kept as a United States historical document. The principles that are delineated in this document were meant to affect the entire African -American populace for 300 years from 1712. Its effectiveness is still evident today. Yet, I believe in our generation, we can see the birth of true liberty as we come to the knowledge of the gospel of Jesus Christ.

Freedom, according to Webster's Dictionary, is a noun that means, "enjoyment of personal liberty; of not being a slave nor a prisoner; the enjoyment of civil rights; freedom of speech; freedom to assemble generally associated with constitutional government; the state of not being subject to determining forces; liberty in action and choosing."

Many people are startled when they hear messages about freedom across the pulpit. They say things like: "Well, why would this be something that has to happen in church? You're talking about freedom and the spirit of the oppressor; shouldn't we just talk about God and spiritualize everything? I think you're getting too political."

One thing I have found is that God is political. If God is not political, He wouldn't have called His mouthpieces to go and speak into the voice of political arenas. Prophets spoke to pharoahs, kings and rulers of nations. I believe that if you're going to be a Christian in this hour, you must become political in your approach. You must address issues.

PROPHETIC PRINCIPLE #3

God is Political!

We must take our heads out of the clouds and focus here on the planet earth. We have been deceived by the enemy in becoming so heavenly minded that we are of no earthly good. We are dealing with real issues. The thing that made the Pharisees and the Sadducees mad is that Jesus dealt with the issues of His day. He challenged the school of traditional thought. He was not afraid to touch the untouchable. He slaughtered the sacred cows of His day. He trumpeted change into ears that had adapted to circumstantial corruption. He did not ignore the societal atmosphere, as most of us do today.

PROPHETIC PRINCIPLE #4

Challenge the school of traditional thought.

Many say, "Don't worry about anything because Jesus is going to come. Don't be concerned with certain issues, just look to Jesus, just make sure that Jesus is the Author and the Finisher of your faith——just love the Lord." However the, Bible lets us know that we are the salt of the earth. You cannot make impact until you make contact.

PROPHETIC PRINCIPLE #5

**You cannot make impact
until you make contact.**

The Bible says that you shall know the truth, and the truth shall make you free (John 8:32). When you understand freedom in the light of liberation, you will find that, as a nation, we have not really experienced freedom in the Kingdom of God.

During slavery, it was unlawful for slaves to meet without whites present. If five or more slaves were to gather, there had to be an overseer present. We are dealing with the same spirit of the age in our generation. If you were to call a meeting and advertise, "Black men only," then you will hear that same spirit which spoke 200 years ago object by saying, "You are a racist. Why are there just black men meeting? Why can't we come? It is dangerous to let too many of you congregate at the same time."

Yet secret societies and other institutions freely gather in America and keep their membership quite exclusive of those they have labeled as "undesirable". Their desire for privacy is respected. Even if you wanted to join, you couldn't. Yet the assembling of black men is seen as threatening to "their civil rights". This will cause you to understand the American concept of freedom in a different light.

It will only be the power of the gospel of Jesus Christ that will bring liberation to men and women. Men have been waiting to hear the gospel that will bring freedom to them as individuals.

PROPHETIC PRINCIPLE #6

The gospel of Jesus Christ will bring liberation.

CHAPTER TWO

CREATED IN HIS IMAGE

"And God said, Let us make man in our image, after our likeness: and let them have dominion over the fish of the sea, and over the fowl of the air, and over the cattle, and over all the earth, and over every creeping thing that creepeth upon the earth."

Genesis 1:26

God said, "Let us make man in our image." The Hebrew word for God is "Elohim," which is a uni-plural noun. The strong and mighty God and the Creator of the universe begins to speak and appoint man in the book of Genesis.

PROPHETIC PRINCIPLE #7

Man is created in the image of God.

The word "said" in the Hebrew means "to command." God commanded, "Let us make man in our image." He didn't make man inferior because he is created in the image of God. Anything that takes man and attempts to redefine his potential into a parody of the image of God is something that is moving against the very creation of God.

PROPHETIC PRINCIPLE #8

The creation of God is never inferior.

God put His Spirit in man so that he can now become a new creature. We must come to understand the new birth, which is to be born from above and to have the Seed of God resident on the inside of us. When you become regenerated, you become re-gened.

PROPHETIC PRINCIPLE #9

Man wasn't created to be a boy.

Man wasn't created to be a boy, or to work for someone else. That is not your ultimate destiny. Black men were created to become producers, creators and inventors, not only entertainers and athletes. God has instilled you with the ability to invent and control entertainment itself. It is time for you to step up. It is not just enough to have your own business or to push someone else's products across the counter. You must become the product that is pushed. You must become the producer of the product.

"Make" means "to do or to create." In the broadest application, it also means, "to accomplish, to advance, to appoint, to become, to commit, to prepare, to procure, to provide." The verb "make" is used in numerous crystalized expressions, and always with the same basic idea. "Asa" is also used in the sense of ethical obligation. It is used in the sense to emphasize the fashioning of an object."

You are in a system that fashioned an object of ridicule, but they didn't make man. That is why you have a hard time finding a man. So many of our men have been psychologically "messed up;" for they came into the hands of a system that was willing to utilize their energy, physical strength and talents, but which refused to see them as men. This is why we must have our own educational systems. We must pull our children out of a corrupt system that is steering them into the pathways of failure.

> *"So God created man in his own image, in the image of God created he him; male and female created he them.*
> *And God blessed them, and God said unto them, Be fruitful, and multiply, and replenish the earth, and subdue it: and have dominion over the fish of the sea, and over the fowl of the air, and over every living thing that moveth upon the earth."*
>
> Genesis 1:27,28

It is time for man to come into the image of God.

PROPHETIC PRINCIPLE #10

Money talks loud and muffles the voice of poverty.

You must become what God has declared you to be. During the 1960's, we were sidetracked by focusing on the issue of Civil Rights. Rights had nothing whatsoever to do with injustice, for if you have wealth, you have rights. Money talks loud and muffles the voice of poverty. We were marching down streets singing, "We shall overcome someday." That was a signal to America's conscience that there was a people in her walls who were not free.

Some people still echo the song in a spirit of sentimentalism instead of perceiving the harsh reality of the conditions of this nation. People need to just wake up and realize that they are not overcomers. That is why the world system will say, "Reverend, you need to speak to spiritual issues, and just concentrate on getting your people free from sin." This is error, for the saving grace of Jesus Christ extends into every issue that affects the entire man. If your message does not address the deliverance of the whole man - spirit, soul, and body - then you are not preaching the gospel of Jesus Christ.

The apostle tells us that it is wrong to go to a man that is hungry and say "Be thou filled." If the man is hungry, don't preach to him the gospel of Jesus until you solve his immediate need. Give him the solution to his problem, then preach the gospel of the Kingdom. Fulfill the man's natural appetite so that you can speak to the appetite for God in his heart.

MALE AND FEMALE
CREATED EQUAL

"Bara" means "create." It carries the thought of the initiation of the object involved. It always connotes what only God can do and frequently emphasizes the absolute newness of the object created. Again, the word "Asa," is much broader in scope, signifying, more or less, "the fashioning of the object with little concern for the special....."

When God said that He created the heavens and the earth, He brought it out of nothing. But when He "made," He shaped and fashioned it into His image. He made man out of the dust of the ground.

When God created man, gender was not given. Man was both male and female. When God said, "Let us make man," He made a male man and a female man. The only difference between a woman (a female man) and a male man is this: a female is a man with a womb.

We have been so Eurocentric in our subjugation of women. In African history, women have ruled nations. The Queen of Sheba was a powerful woman. She didn't appear before Solomon with a book of food stamps. She was a Queen. In African culture, you have many nations that women spearheaded, yet it took nothing away from their men. Both were equally strong and intelligent.

The subjugation of women is not a tradition of God. The Bible scholars conferred about the book of Esther, and debated its authenticity and relevance to be included in the Bible. Was the real discussion because God's Name wasn't mentioned or was it because it was named after a woman? It is the only book in the Bible that is named after a woman. Could it be that because we have become so Eurocentric in our thoughts, we have picked up their culture and philosophy until we began to enslave anything that was not controlled by the white male? How do we perceive our women...our queens?

PROPHETIC PRINCIPLE #II

**The subjugation of women
is not a tradition of God.**

I am convinced that Christianity became perverted when Rome became involved. The Scripture confirms that Africans were at the head of the church before Christianity reached the ears of Rome. Women were used of God.

> *This is the book of the generations of Adam. In the day that God created man, in the likeness of God made he him;*
>
> *Male and female created he them; and blessed them, and called their name Adam, in the day when they were created.*
>
> Genesis 5:1,2

This means that Eve's real name was Adam. Adam wasn't just a man, but a race of people. If we, as a people, ever get our men to walk in the image of God that He created, we will be a mighty race, a mighty nation that will begin to bring forth the Kingdom of God in our generation.

I am not for the suppression of our women. I am strongly against it. Yes, our women are strong. Yes, our women have controlled the family. Yes, our women have picked up the slack. Yes, our women have generated income. No, I don't want you to take a back seat, women, but rather, I want you to keep maintaining your status! For when black men come into their destiny and begin to become one with their women again, we will see a mighty nation coming forth!

MAN - THE DIVINE WILL OF GOD

The creation of man was preceded by the Divine consultation of God the Father, God the Son, and God the Holy Ghost. God said, "Let us make man." The only time that God called a counsel together during the creation was when He was ready to make man. Counsel was divine; held by the three Persons of the Trinity, whose thought was expressed in the image of man.

The consultation was solemn. The light, the water, the dry land, the heavenly bodies, and the spirit world had all heard and obeyed the Voice of God. But no consultation had been held prior to their entrance into the world. Why? Because they were matter; dumb, impotent, and devoid of the image of God. Now God is creating a being endowed with a mind and independent volition who will have the unique ability to choose between obedience to and defiance against Him — "Let us make man."

PROPHETIC PRINCIPLE #12

It is impossible for an anointed person to be silent.

The book of Genesis is the book of beginnings. Our

nation, which specializes in oppression, utilizes media and the corporate setting to shape an entire race into an image that is a parody of the image of God.

When we understand what is happening with our black males, the Church can't be silent. To walk around waiting to meet Jesus in the sky is hypocritical. It is impossible for an anointed person, filled with the Holy Spirit, to be silent. To be silent is "to be in agreement with." Therefore, there must be prophetic voices that become the voices of those who are held captive by want. There must become prophetic voices that will speak forth the Word of the Lord in truth and in power.

In this hour, we are finding that very few people want to be prophets after this order. Many that have walked with me at Zoe Ministries say, "We have enjoyed the prophetic. You have prophesied concerning my check. You have prophesied concerning my job. You have prophesied concerning my career, and you told me what classes to take. I can hear the Word of the Lord in those areas. But this Word that you are bringing now is cutting, and it's sharp. I don't know if this is the Word of the Lord."

Why? To deny this as being the Word of the Lord

PROPHETIC PRINCIPLE #13

Prophets never won popularity contests.

is to deny everything that God has spoken through the prophetic Voice of the Lord in Zoe Ministries. Is it that it is not the Word of the Lord, or is it that we don't want to face the ugliness of our deeds and the atrocity of our sin? Until we can acknowledge that corruption exists and that we are in a system that is ungodly, we can't bring about change; neither can we become part of the answer, but we will continue to part of the problem.

PROPHETIC PRINCIPLE #14

**Words of correction can place
you back in right standing with God!**

The prophets of God in the Scripture were never very popular. Usually the masses were against the message because when the prophets spoke the Word of the Lord, they disturbed kingdoms and structures. They didn't just go around saying, "The Lord is getting ready to touch you financially. The Lord is going to do something in your marriage — just lift your hands and worship Him right now."

The prophets of old would declare, "Thus saith the Lord..." and the Word of the Lord would come forth to correct that which was wrong and make it right. That

is righteousness; bringing things into the right align-
ment, into the right order as God has declared it
should be.

We have grown up believing lies. Everything
around us has been a lie. From the images that we
have been taught to bow to within the Catholic
Church, to the picture of Jesus that is sitting on your
grandmother's wall. Everything around us has been a
lie, and trouble is agitated whenever you walk in the
image of God to bring truth. When you start turning
lights on within the minds of the populace that expose
the deception of the world system, you become a
marked individual.

PROPHETIC PRINCIPLE #15

**Walking in the image of
God will expose the enemy!**

When you start telling people to destroy the photos of their white Jesus, a faction of society will rise up
to say, "There is neither black nor white. We don't look
at color." Good, well then, let's base the image of
Christ upon that which is given within the Scriptures
and destroy the white Jesus photos. We have been
beholding a lie that doesn't add up.

There are people who have problems with the African Heritage Bible. A man of God asked me, "You have been preaching this message concerning liberation of the black man, but I don't know if the people are ready for this, it really doesn't take all that, it is really not necessary so why don't you go back to preaching some of the other things that can be understood?" I responded, "This is not something new that we are making up, we are only preaching truth. What are you saying? Stay away from the truth and go back to the lie that you have been preaching to us?"

PROPHETIC PRINCIPLE #16

Liberation speak Truth!
Fear and Compromise speak Lies!

Many of us want to see the Christ, but what God wants to do is point us to Jesus of Nazareth — the liberator. Nathaniel didn't have a problem with Jesus, but he had a problem with Jesus' origin.

The Jews had a hard time receiving Jesus because He didn't come in the package that they were looking for. In this hour, God is wrapping America's deliverance in despised packaging that will offend many.

PROPHETIC PRINCIPLE #17

Focus on CONTENT - not WRAPPING!

There is a cry for truth that emanates from the deepest chambers of the heart of man. Someone told me that some whites in a particular state were so upset by my message that they declared I would not be allowed to return to their state to preach——(as if they hold the keys to the airports). They are trying to determine my destiny and where the Word of the Lord will go. Who *are* they to tell me where my plane will land?

There is a force that is attempting to keep you under control. You may ask, "Is this message necessary?" Yes, because the truth will make you free. I am just trying to get you ready for heaven. Then when you see Jesus with His afro, you won't get upset! We are just attempting to prepare you in advance. You won't ask the Father, "Is this the one or do we look for another?"

PROPHETIC PRINCIPLE #18

Don't be controlled by a lie!

When people say, "I have a difficult time with this message," it is because most people sit in church and never have experienced conviction. It is the first time you have ever been convicted. This is why people could go to church, sit comfortably, and still have signs on their walls that said, "No coloreds allowed."

PROPHETIC PRINCIPLE #19

If you have not been convicted in Church, then the Truth is not in the message!

No one preached a message that brought conviction for the sin of tampering with the image of God. They were able to do whatever they pleased and the preacher would smile in their face and say, "God bless you! Send me an offering today, for we are here to bless you!" They were probably some of the same preachers whose grandparents or parents, or even themselves had hoods on in the night. The chairman of the deacon board had white sheets in the back of his car. They were singing, "Bringing in the sheaves" while castrating black men and raping black women.

PROPHETIC PRINCIPLE #20

A lie wants to cover itself!

I could go into white churches and preach a message that would identify with the making of a boy, instead of the making of a man. As long as we don't talk about the redistribution of power, everything is fine. There is a redistribution of power when we take individuals who have the mindset of a male and let them know that God has made you a man, God has made you a husband and God has made you a father.

When you raise up fathers, you are raising up generations. Why is there a crying out in this area? Because I am afraid that if voices do not emerge from the Church by the turn of the Century, what we call "freedom" today may become concentration camps tomorrow.

American history started so innocently. The Indians and the white men were eating together, exchanging gifts; perhaps even eating turkey together, and sharing blankets. After this glorious time of fellowship and trust, the white men forged a trail of tears that blazed across the nation. Don't say it can't happen today!

If there is not a hearing ear of people who will hearken to the prophets of God, slavery can happen. Usually when any people want to oppress another people, they remove the priest, the prophet, the eyes, and the seer. If they pluck out the eyes of a culture, it will remain in darkness and blindness. It takes a prophet to lead you out.

PROPHETIC PRINCIPLE #21

**Generations will be saved by
the raising up of fathers.**

The Church fought prophetic voices because certain men wished to have the final word on such matters. If a prophet emerges among you, he will be your eyes. He will lead you out of Egypt, through the wilderness, and into your promised land.

PROPHETIC PRINCIPLE #22

**When hearing and seeing ceases,
bondage is imminent!**

The seer is the eyes of the community. This is why we encourage people to enroll in The School of the Prophets where they learn to hear the Voice of God. We must interpret the Scriptures; not in the light of European theologians, but we must go to the Word of God expecting Him to show us the truth.

The truth has been colored. The face of the truth has literally been changed. Jesus said, "I am The Way. I am The Truth." Truth is not a philosophy, but rather truth is a Person. The face of Truth has been changed. Truth comes in the image of the oppressed, not the oppressors. The face of Truth has been changed, which means that we have been following a lie, mesmerized by something that looks like the Truth.

PROPHETIC PRINCIPLE #23

Locating the Prophet will bring you into the Canaan Land!

It is like a story that was once told: The Truth took off his clothes and was taking a swim. The Lie was sneaking around, stole Truth's clothes and ran through town. People looked and said, "That looks like The Truth." Suddenly, the Truth came running, chasing behind the Lie and the people watching said, "But that's The Naked Truth."

People had been previously following that which looked like the truth, but now they are receiving the naked truth. Undress the lie!!

People have been following some ideologies that their great-grandmother, their great-great-grand-mother, and their great-great-great-great-great-grand-mother followed. People still have a photo of a white Jesus on their walls. Oppressed people can't identify with it. You are dealing with this type of image in your mind. It is hard to relate to God in the light that He is normally presented. If I believed in this system, I would think that God was against black people.

PROPHETIC PRINCIPLE #24

Your oppressor will disfigure the face of Truth!

Criminals go to court and place their hands on the Bible in a system that is unjust. It is no wonder when they get into prison, they turn away from Christianity and embrace Islam. We, as preachers of the gospel, fail to undress the lie and tell the truth.

PROPHETIC PRINCIPLE #25

Unjust systems turn the hearts of men away from God!

CREATED TO RULE

You were not created to be oppressed by another people. That is not the image of God. The image of God is that you would have dominion and rule as God in the earth!

The devil won't like you when you start walking in the image of God because you will stand erect. A slave would get whipped for looking his master in the eyes. Why was he whipped? He would be judged for being a man. He was judged for becoming the image of God. When you understand the mindset of the religious leaders of that day, you'll discover that they really didn't want you to have the Bible in your hands. When they did give you the Book, they were reading the Scriptures to you. Some held their services in Latin, with the hopes that you wouldn't master the language and thus remain ignorant.

PROPHETIC PRINCIPLE #26

When you walk in the image of God your oppressor will judge you!

The theologians compiled several texts to interpret the Scriptures for you. You wouldn't dare go against what they said. We were afraid to challenge the very system that was designed to enslave us, instead of freeing us.

PROPHETIC PRINCIPLE #27

**Fools fear systems.
Liberators challenge them!**

and said, "You can just give them the Book anyway because they are not going to read it." How do you know that? Because there are many people who walk out of my local church service and don't pick up any of my books!

You say, "Pastor, I need counseling." I ask, "What is wrong with you?" You say, "I am having money problems." I ask, "Do you have my book, "The Power of Money?" You say, "No." I ask, "Well, why don't you get my book? Why don't you get the tape series and materials that thoroughly cover that area. Why do I have to reteach it to you when we already have it in recorded or book form? If you are too lazy to read, then pop the tape in a cassette and play it while you sleep. Maybe your subconscious will catch it and tip it over into your conscious mind."

PROPHETIC PRINCIPLE #28

Liberators embrace knowledge! Laziness may be the cause of your present situation!

Something happens when you start searching the Scriptures. We should have known that it wasn't the gospel that we were receiving because the Bible says, "Where the Spirit of the Lord is there is liberty." You haven't experienced liberty in certain churches, so you should have known that the Spirit of the Lord was not there!

CREATED TO INCREASE

The universe was God's gift to man. It was designed for the occupation of man. God put this universe here for us to enjoy. It was presented to Adam. Nature, from its highest manifestation to its lowest, was to minister to his happiness and to his needs. The universe was created for you, not for someone to tell you where you could and couldn't go; not for anyone to say you can live here, but you can't live there.

God created a man to walk on this planet, to be in His image and likeness. He wanted to show His affection and love for man. He created man to increase. Everyday the gift is increasing in value. The longer you hold some things, the more valuable they become. Your life should become more valuable.

PROPHETIC PRINCIPLE #29

If you have depreciated in value then you are not walking in the image and likeness of God.

The longer you live, the wiser you should become. We don't value life in our own community. We don't even have insurance on our lives. An insurance broker told me that a person should be insured 10 times his income. He said, "If you are not insured ten times your income, you are under insured." For example, if you make $30,000 a year, you should have a minimum of $3,000,000 dollars of insurance that you are leaving to empower those you leave behind.

Some of us will only purchase $10,000 dollars worth of insurance. Many of our grandparents only paid a nickel a month for insurance. How much is your life worth? If the individual dies prematurely, what value has been taken out of your life?

In the face of these harsh realities, we must open our eyes to recognize that there is a demonic move to destroy our black males. Everytime a male dies, particularly a young male in his warrior years (between 13 to 25), we have lost the years of his greatest strength. We have lost their warrior years, where they were to accumulate knowledge and strength, and set the ground level for their businesses and empires. Instead, their minds are being indoctrinated to the prison of societal slavery, and captivity becomes an austere certainty to those who are entrapped by their frustrated cravings.

We must preach a gospel that liberates. We must preach a gospel where men and women can understand that prison is not the rite of passage for the black community to prove that you are a man or woman. We must become a people of economic empowerment. Parents, when you lose a son that is 30 years old, 20 years old, or 15 years old, you have lost your social security, for God's plan was for your children to take care of you in your old age. When society scoffs at the death of our youth, they mock those that remain, and denigrate our humanity.

PROPHETIC PRINCIPLE #30

God created children to be their parents' "Social Security".

God created man to increase. God created man so that He could show him His love. One of the greatest objects of creation was to manifest the love of God to the human race. It was brought into existence - the lights, the sun, the stars, the creation and the creation of man. All of these were the love token of God. These were designed not to display His power and His wisdom, but His desire for the happiness of man. God created you to be happy, and gave you an appetite for truth.

The world is a great school. Solomon said, "Go to the ant to learn wisdom." You can learn by beholding nature. Everything that you need to understand and know is able to be perceived in nature if you open your eyes to behold truth. "...Thou sluggard" — lazy people — go to the ant! Notice how ants gather in the summer so that they can relax when winter appears.

As a people, we must look at the ant. Stop living for today and prepare for your future. Don't try to exist upon instant gratification. You must learn how to pay yourself. Pay 10 percent in tithes, 10 percent offerings, pay yourself 10 percent, and live off of the 70 percent. You should give the 10 percent that you pay yourself an assignment to begin to go and work on your behalf to bring back a return.

PROPHETIC PRINCIPLE #31

Instant gratification is designed for fools.

If you don't pay yourself 10 percent every week, you are a slave. You have no self-worth. If you can't afford to pay yourself, then you are no different than those who came out of slavery. This is a basic principle that will lead you to economic liberty.

Slaves came through the period of reconstruction where they were trying to get their lives together. Everyone rejoiced when the slaves were freed. Now, they were given the opportunity to begin sharecropping, but they couldn't pay themselves. They went to work; they worked hard, but they couldn't pay themselves. The "massa" changed his face from the slavemaster to the employer. An individual who works for food, clothes and shelter is just working for survival. You are poor when you are working for money. Living from paycheck to paycheck is slavery. But when you are able to exercise wisdom and force money to work for you, then you have reached a place of real wealth and economic empowerment.

PROPHETIC PRINCIPLE #32

Economic Empowerment will lead you out of bondage.

CHAPTER THREE
THE FASHIONED MAN

When I consider thy heavens, the work of thy fingers, the moon and the stars, which thou hast ordained.;

What is man, that thou art mindful of him? and the son of man, that thou visitest him?

For thou hast made him a little lower than the angels, and hast crowned him with glory and honour.

Thou madest him to have dominion over the works of thy hands; thou hast put all things under his feet.

Psalms 8:3-6

PROPHETIC PRINCIPLE #33

You were created to dominate!

"For thou has made him a little lower than angels...." (Psalm 8:5). In the Hebrew, the word "angels" means, "a little lower than Elohim," a little lower than God. Maybe the translators couldn't handle the fact that God would make man a little lower than Him, so they recorded the word as angels.

Man has been made in the image and likeness of God, especially when you have been born again. The Seed from above is in you. That is why you can now say, "I am a new creature in Christ Jesus, old things are passed away and behold all things are become new." Because I have been born from above, that means that now I have the power to become.

The Bible says "for as many as believe on Him, they shall become sons of God." This is why slave owners debated as to whether they would expose slaves to the fullness of Christianity. They thought that if they gave them the Bible, they would become liberated because the truth will make you free. This is why they took the lie and dressed it up like the truth and let them follow that which looked like the truth. Blacks have been taught that they should not get involved in politics and government. Some of you still believe that. The Holy Ghost is challenging your entire belief system!

PROPHETIC PRINCIPLE #34

True Christians will speak the Truth!

Some of you are saying, "Prophet, just leave it alone, because it comes with too many problems, just let it go, why don't you just let it rest and preach about heaven? Your message isn't edifying!" People want me to talk about, "I got shoes, you got shoes, all God's children got shoes! And when I get to heaven I'm going to put on my shoes; I am going to shout all over God's heaven!"

When you begin to read the Bible, you will find that the Bible doesn't make much reference to heaven. The Bible is an earth book, not a heaven book. Take your head out of the heavens and begin to address what is going on in the earth!

We love singing about heaven, "We are going to walk around heaven all day." We even sing, "If you live right, heaven belongs to you. If you pray right, heaven belongs to you. Oh, heaven belongs to you. If you shout right, heaven belongs to you."

These songs depicted inaccurate information because if you live right, the earth shall belong to you. The meek shall inherit the earth! But the oppressor said, "Just keep those good little children shouting about heaven, get a good tune to it and let it feel good, and they'll be dancing all night." They will dance themselves into a frenzy and become so intoxicated by the "spirit" until they will not address real issues; they will not be able to become prophets to their generation because they will not address issues — just keep them looking towards heaven.

PROPHETIC PRINCIPLE #35

The oppressor wants you to focus on heaven while God is saying inherit the earth!

This is why I don't preach a lot about heaven in my local assembly. I don't talk too much about the rapture of the Church. Many have attempted to interpret the book of Revelation and force the visions to fit new technological developments. Oppressors have taught that the computer is the "beast" — but that was just their way of keeping you away from information; keeping you ignorant. Ignorant people become enslaved people because knowledge is power. If the computer was the beast, then how are all of their materials being printed and mailed to you?

They change computer equipment every three to six months, just to keep you out of the know. Number one, they know that you can't afford it. Secondly, you are too lazy to open up the book and read it. They just keep moving on and progressing. You are just now getting an understanding of the electric typewriter. You are still working with word processors, instead of getting into the computer age and being in the know. This is why Jesus said, "The children of darkness are wiser in their generation than the children of light." It is time to take the blinders off!

PROPHETIC PRINCIPLE #36

Step out of old mindsets and leap into the future.

THE EXPRESS IMAGE OF GOD

The fowl of the air, and the fish of the sea, and what-soever passeth through the paths of the seas.

O Lord our Lord, how excellent is thy name in all the earth!

Psalms 8:8,9

PROPHETIC PRINCIPLE #37

Be wiser than your oppressor!

Many scholars believe that God's image doesn't exist in man's body which was formed from the earthly matter. Some say that it wasn't the natural image. But if God said that He made man in His "image," for some reason, He started forming His image in a continent that we know today as Africa. For some reason that is where He began creation.

God created the original man in the continent of Africa. He had to start with some big noses when He blew into man's nostrils. He was blowing nations in him. He was blowing lives into him, so He had to get the largest nostrils. He blew into His nostrils the breath of life and man became a living soul. To my African brethren: Don't be ashamed of your nose, for you are fearfully and wonderfully made!

PROPHETIC PRINCIPLE #38

Creation began in Africa!

You must understand some things concerning oppression: when the oppressor comes, he takes your knowledge. Usually they burn the libraries in order to burn your culture. They burn your source of information. Therefore, you feel as though you have been inferior people, but you were heart surgeons, architects, scientists and geniuses! You are recorded in the Scriptures!

PROPHETIC PRINCIPLE #39

We were created to be people of integrity!

Don't let anyone tell you that Christianity is a white man's religion, for that is far from the truth. We were in the gospel before Europe was. It was a black man who carried the cross of Jesus. The crowd was unruly, having just insisted that Barabbas be released and Jesus be crucified. When Jesus collapsed under the strain of carrying the cross, they sought for someone who looked just like Him, to satisfy the rage of the crowd. How much closer can you get? Mary and Joseph took Jesus into Egypt to hide. How can you hide, unless you can blend in?

PROPHETIC PRINCIPLE #40

We were the true originators of the Word of God - Not the white man!

Peter was talking about people of color when he said "Let it not be the outward adorning, the apparel..." because you know how we dress when we get ready to go to church! "Don't let it be the plaiting of your hair..." Don't let anyone tell you that you were not in Scripture! Even the Ethiopian eunuch was coming from Jerusalem because he was a Jew. God interrupted a revival that was taking place and took Philip into the desert to begin to open up the eyes of the Ethiopian eunuch. Don't tell me that we were not there from the beginning! This is not a white man's religion — we were there from the beginning! There is no such continent called "The Middle East." When you are dealing with a system that has been operating in lies, they will dress the lie up as the truth. You have to undress the lie. They called it "Middle East" because they didn't want the land identified with Africa.

We must wonder; if Moses grew up in Egypt and looked like the Egyptians, and if Solomon said I am black and comely (who was also a Jew) and if Jesus was a Jew whose parents took Him to Egypt, and if Jesus has the blood of the Father who placed the divine seed in Mary and Jesus is the image of the Father and His hair is like wool and His feet is as bronze.... If we believe in the virgin birth.....then we are faced with an identity crisis, and we must dethrone the lie!!!

PROPHETIC PRINCIPLE #41

Your oppressor will cause you to have an identity crisis.

I beheld till the thrones were cast down, and the Ancient of days did sit, whose garment was white as snow, and the hair of his head like the pure wool: his throne was like the fiery flame, and his wheels as burning fire.

Daniel 7:9

Jesus' hair was like pure wool. For some reason, God allowed these things to be recorded. Perhaps, in His omniscience, He knew that there were a people to be born whose beauty would be denied for 300 years. God caused Jesus to come in the image of a people that would be despised.

And above the firmament that was over their heads was the likeness of a throne, as the appearance of a sapphire stone: and upon the likeness of the throne was the likeness as the appearance of a man above upon it.

Ezekiel 1:26

If you don't think that color matters, then why did you paint the lie?

Who being the brightness of his glory, and the express image of his person, and upholding all things by the word of his power, when he had by himself purged our sins, sat down on the right hand of the Majesty on high.

Hebrews 1:3

PROPHETIC PRINCIPLE #42

Color is significant to God!

You have to come in touch with who Jesus is. Islam is not a religion for black people and neither is Christianity a white man's religion. If someone had informed them of this a generation ago, we wouldn't have to go through this now.

We were not "Johnny Come Lately," but rather, we were in creation from the beginning. Moses was black. When God got through with Abram, He stuck "ham" at the end of his name! Abram is the father of black people, and in him all the nations would be blessed.

PROPHETIC PRINCIPLE #43

Blessings flow through the Black Nation!

You can't get black out of white, but you can get white out of black. In "him" all nations would be blessed. Everything had to start in Africa. Africa was the source of civilization in the world. Don't believe the Tarzan movies! Your ancestors were never "jungle bunnies!" Hollywood has messed up your thinking!

And I turned to see the voice that spake with me. And being turned, I saw seven golden candlesticks;

And in the midst of the seven candlesticks one like unto the Son of man, clothed with a garment down to the foot, and girt about the paps with a golden girdle.

His head and his hairs were white like wool, as white as snow; and his eyes were as a flame of fire;

And his feet like unto fine brass, as if they burned in a furnace; and his voice as the sound of many waters.

Revelation 1:12-15

How could this be? Somehow God allowed His Son to come, who was the express image of His Father. The texture of Jesus' hair wasn't different from His Father's hair. If we believe in the Immaculate Conception, then we must believe that the seed of the Father went into Mary and God is sitting in heaven as a black man.

PROPHETIC PRINCIPLE #44

Jesus was a black man!

The paintings of black Madonnas and black Christs are traceable to time before the 14th, 15th, and 16th centuries. In 1505, Pope Julius II commissioned Michaelangelo to start painting a replacement. "We don't like the picture of this black Mary and this black Jesus, can you paint Jesus so that He looks like us?" Michaelangelo was followed by Leonardo DaVinci, Rafael and others. They changed the image of the Christ.

PROPHETIC PRINCIPLE #45

Restoring the image of God will anger your oppressor!

We have to lay hands on our artists and tell them to get the image back. Are you making Jesus black? No. That is what He was originally. We are just restoring the image. Are you angry with us because we're restoring the image?

Man, who was created out of soil, began in Africa, and God named him "Adam." He was not just a man, but he was going to be a race of people. He was a man full of color. We all know what color dirt is, so we can imagine Adam's true form.

Some people will ask, "What difference does it make?" Well, if you are going to have a photo hanging on your wall, then let's get as close to the right image on your wall as possible!

PROPHETIC PRINCIPLE #46

Stop hanging a white Jesus on your wall!

We are bringing an awareness to the consciousness of the Church. My mission is to speak to the Church, to a people and to a nation. During the earlier part of the century, we could not have had signs in America that said, "whites only," if it was not already being said in the Church. We could not have had signs saying, "No coloreds allowed," unless it were first permitted in the Church. The world becomes a reflection of what is already existing in the Church.

Store owners of that era went to church at 11:00 a.m. on Sunday morning. Those very same citizens and government leaders went to church and worshipped God, with their Bible under their arms. They even sang hymns, "A Mighty Fortress is our God, ..." They sang the hymns, but yet there was not a gospel that was being preached that brought conviction to the heart — they did not hear the gospel of the Kingdom.

If they were aware of the gospel of the Kingdom, then there would have been a change in their actions. I'm forced to also venture out and say that "neither was the Spirit of the Lord moving in their midst." If the Spirit of the Lord had been moving while the slaves were worshipping, they would have been liberated. Wherever the Spirit of the Lord is, there is liberty (II Corinthians 3:17). The Holy Ghost would have showed up in the message and slave masters would have said, "I can't enslave you any longer, for the Spirit of the Lord is here."

PROPHETIC PRINCIPLE #47

The Spirit of the Lord brings liberty!

Now we must ask, "What kind of spirit has been going around in the Church? It has not been a spirit that has been sent of God because the Spirit of the

Lord would liberate. There are theologians, men of God who are preaching to blacks, who still believe that blacks were the descedants of Ham and cursed by God. Some still believe that blacks were elected to be slaves. They say, "One day the curse will be lifted off of you; you just be good boys and girls and you will see."

Our youth are questioning in their minds whether or not God is a racist. They can't help but ask, "Does God like black people?" And to think that there are those who do not wish this message to be preached....for shame!

PROPHETIC PRINCIPLE #48

You are NOT cursed!

BECOMING PRODUCERS

Genesis 1:27-28
"So God created man in his own image, in the image of God created he him; male and female created he them. And God blessed them, and God said unto them, Be fruitful, and multiply, and replenish the earth, and subdue it: and have dominion over the fish of the sea, and over the fowl of the air, and over every living thing that moveth upon the earth."

God blessed them.

Again, the female wasn't created to be walked on by the male. When we hear this message on liberation, we are not only going to see the liberation of the black male, but a liberation of women as well.

The Church of England is beginning now to welcome women in ministry to function as priests. Now, we are going to begin to see God's manifestation in the house of God, in the image of God which is male and female. Whenever there is only one side, it becomes slanted, perverted and distorted. You need male and female in order to produce life.

God blessed Adam and Eve and said, "...be fruitful...." God is telling you today to be fruitful and multiply. He wants you to begin to reproduce and increase.

PROPHETIC PRINCIPLE #49

God is a liberator of male and female!

The word "fruitful" means, "to bear fruit; to bring forth; to grow; to increase." God has created us to increase. It is the devil's job to decrease you. It is God's job to increase you.

When you begin to walk in the image and likeness of God, you are going to increase; you are going to be fruitful; you are going to multiply; you are going to replenish the earth and subdue it. It is time for us to become producers. It is time for us to stop being field hands and staff people in our oppressor's corporations. It is time for us to run our own corporations and empires; it is time for us to create cars and products. We need to start producing things in our society that will bring economic empowerment to ourselves first and then to others.

We, as the Church of the Lord Jesus Christ, must go back to a message where we teach our black men and women to love themselves. When they get into the educational system, they are taught not to love themselves. They're taught that their history evolved from cannabalistic savages, and are forced to sit shamefaced as their humanity is humiliated.

PROPHETIC PRINCIPLE #50

Empower your community FIRST!

For some reason, most people think that black history began at 1619; at the time of slavery. We had a history thousands of years before then. When others in the world were uncivilized, you were civilized. Kings and queens were reigning in Africa while other cultures were still living in caves.

PROPHETIC PRINCIPLE #5I

Royalty is the beginning of our history, NOT slavery!

There has to be a renewing of the mind. The Apostle Paul lets us know the key to transformation, "I beseech you therefore, brethren, by the mercies of God that ye present your bodies a living sacrifice, holy, acceptable unto God, which is your reasonable service. And be not conformed to this world: but be ye transformed by the renewing of your mind, that ye may prove what is that good, and acceptable, and perfect, will of God" (Romans 12:1,2).

In other words, don't be conformed to the system that you are in. Don't be conformed to the environment that is trying to teach you that your "rite of passage" is to be beaten by a cop and be thrown into prison. Your "rite of passage," young lady, is not to get pregnant as a teenager. You must not conform to the system of this world, but you must be transformed by the renewing of your mind.

PROPHETIC PRINCIPLE #52

Systems were created to enslave you!

Whites have not been trained to address issues in black people. They can't speak for us — (this must be understood) — because they don't understand the struggle that we have been through as a people. When they talk to you, they talk down to you. It is difficult for them to identify, unless they walk away from their community and pick up what the struggle is about today (which is the cross of Jesus) by identifying with oppressed people.

Jesus didn't deliver mankind by staying in the heavens. The only way that He could deliver man was by becoming one with him. When He came, He came in the earth as a homeless individual. He wasn't born in a palace or in the suburbs. If we look at it today, the 20th Century, He would have been born walking the streets with Mary and Joseph in Harlem, and they would have gone to one of the shelters and said, "Is there any room?" They would have been homeless victims of a present day system.

You can't be a deliverer of a people until you become a victim of a system. That is why I can stand boldly and say, "Blacks have no business under white pastors as leaders." You may think, "That is racism." No it isn't. They can't deliver you. They can't give you what is needed because they were never victims. What you are experiencing there is not a move of God, but cultural surrender. You are guilty of denying who you are, what you are, and never becoming what God has ordained for you to become.

PROPHETIC PRINCIPLE #53

Never deny who you really are!

You are trying to become something that you are not. When you enter into worship, you lose your dance, your movement, and you become stiff. When you talk to others you say foolish things like, "It doesn't take all of that. All of that is not necessary."

You have to become connected to what God has created in you. You must understand that Africa is a spiritual continent. When you begin to identify with the spirituality that is in your culture and bring it into the right standing in which that God has ordained it to be, you become a powerful people. There is something about your movement, about your dance that is unique, and, contrary to the teachings of many of our charismatic white brethren, it is not demonic!

PROPHETIC PRINCIPLE #54

You've been created for uniqueness!

There is something that is in your speech; perhaps you haven't been to the universities, but when the Spirit of God starts to move in you, you have a way of speaking that brings conviction to the very core of men's souls. There is something about your singing that is spiritual. They will tell you, "That is not proper style. You are going to lose your voice in about seven years." But, there is a color in your voice, an arrangement that others can't quite pick out. Why?

Because a people have gotten in touch with themselves and haven't walked away from what God has put on the inside of them!

There is something about your dance that is unique. You were told that you couldn't take up ballet because you didn't have the proper physique, but there is something about your dance when you are not trying to be like others!

PROPHETIC PRINCIPLE #55
Be Yourself!

We are in a society that is trying to destroy us. It is trying to get us to give up our culture. The careers of many of our black models are in question when they want to identify with their ability to emphasize their African heritage. Therefore, our models are forced to abandon the uniqueness of the texture of their hair, and culturally assimilate with long weaves and bleached skin to attain longevity and desirability from those who hold the purse strings in that arena.

PROPHETIC PRINCIPLE #56
Imitation is false representation!

Don't tell me that we are not in a society that is trying to get you to give up and surrender your culture; surrender what you are and who you are to become something that you are not. You must get in touch with yourself.

I am not teaching racism. I am teaching my people how to be what God has created them to be. I would be just as wrong if I tried to take whites and mold them into something that they are not. It would be wrong if I tried to get them to speak like us, to sing like us, and to dance like us. It would be wrong if I made any white try to become black. God wants you to keep the uniqueness of what He has made you to be.

You were created to have dominion. You were created to be somebody. Again, Civil Rights was not the issue in the 60's freedom movement. Economic empowerment and real estate was important because when you have wealth, you have rights. What is freedom without the gold to maintain your freedom?

PROPHETIC PRINCIPLE #57

Freedom cannot exist without wealth!

The prevention of the emergence of Moses' strong anointed leadership was the thing that maintained slavery amongst us. The same system was attacked, the same people were going forth, but when Moses came forth and said to Pharaoh, "Let my people go," deliverance came. They are trying to kill off the Moses', for they are the ones with the Word of the Lord to address this system; Let My people go!!

CHAPTER FOUR

THE WORLD'S SYSTEM

All the enemy has to do is keep you from trusting one another. He has created distrust in our community which will cause us to remain impoverished.

We live in a system that has gone against the instructions of God. The Father, Son, and Holy Ghost were all present at creation when God said, "Let us make man in our image." God wanted man to be made in their image, not in the image of angels, for man has been created a little higher than the angels.

We live in a system that says, "Let us make a negro." In other words, let us make a nigger. But God said, "Let us make man," not a boy. We live in a society that refuses to give your mother and father respect by calling them Mr. and Mrs., but instead, they call them uncle and aunt.

PROPHETIC PRINCIPLE #58

System thinking calls us "Niggers."
God's thinking calls us "Men."

We live in a world system that dehumanizes us as individuals and as a black race of people. Recently, and quite unfortunately, the news reported that certain Jews were shot. Within 24 hours, the police claimed that they found a suspect. My brother was killed last year and various city agencies have the report of the police officers that were on the scene, of the bus driver with whom there was a confrontation , and of the ambulance driver that had taken him in to the hospital, and yet they still haven't found a suspect. We still haven't seen a report. Why is that? Because they do not view African life as human and do not see our men as men. When we are killed under suspicious circumstances, the first thing that is looked at is our lifestyle and reputation. They do not feel as strong a need for justice because subconsciously, it is thought that black men deserve to die, for they are as animals in their sight.

PROPHETIC PRINCIPLE #59

Your oppressor will have no regard for black life.

What does this have to do with Church? An alcoholic can't be healed until he first admits that he has a problem. I can't begin ministering about liberation until we bring the problem to the table, and admit that there is a problem. We must first admit that the government is a system which just a dim reflection of what exists in the Church.

God said, "Let us make man." God is into making men after His image and likeness. In New York City alone, statistics show we have more than 80 percent African-American men in prison. We are not all committing crimes. We only make up more than 30 percent of the population, yet we represent 80 percent or more of the prison population. It doesn't take great mathematical skill to realize that these figures just don't add up!

When we look at our rate of imprisonment, homelessness, and joblessness, we must begin to ask the question: Who are the real criminals? Who is the law made for? Mike Tyson received a six year sentence for a dubious crime, but a particular politician's relative only received a rebuke when accused of the same thing. You didn't even have to snatch the bag. It could have been alleged that you snatched the bag and it's almost guaranteed that you will serve time behind bars. You have individuals who cost us billions of dollars in taxes; individuals who have robbed us because of the Savings and Loan scandal, yet how many of them went to prison?

PROPHETIC PRINCIPLE #60

The law serves the oppressor and enslaves the oppressed.

I am finding that law and order is really designed for only certain groups of people. Christianity came to put you in line. We have a police department in our city that has nothing better to do on Sunday mornings than to ticket law-abiding citizen's cars parked in front of the church. Think about the psychology of this. They're letting you know that they think you are in the wrong neighborhood.

We are in a system that doesn't want you to be free as men. "Jim Crowism" is very much alive today — it never died. Someone told me that there is a certain place in Texas where you can gas up your vehicle, but can't spend the night — racism never died. It is still alive. If you don't believe it, then let a black man date a white woman — he has just committed a crime in the sight of some people. If he were to drive through certain places in the South, then he would find this to be true. And if he drove at night, he may not escape with his life.

DEPROGRAMMING THE PROGRAMMING

We live in a world system that is designed for enslavement. We must keep our children away from television. Television programs do just that; they program your mind. It depicts most blacks in a negative light. It has shaped the opinion of the community.

PROPHETIC PRINCIPLE #61

Media can enslave your mind!

Media has said that Malcolm X was a violent man and you believed it. More people died with Martin Luther King and his struggle for civil rights than with Malcolm X. Churches were bombed. People died, had dogs released on them, and torrents of water hosed on them. You didn't have that with Malcolm, but the media always led you to believe that Malcolm was violent. Media has the ability to mutate your opinion to a characterization of their choosing.

If the media came up with a scandal about me today, you would believe it instead of saying, "I know the man. He spoke into my life. I have watched his life. He has a love for his people." But as soon as they come you will say, "I told you, I knew something was wrong because Channel X said it, or the Daily Lie wrote it." You must stop believing everything the media says!!

Media is controlled by the oppressor. They control the images that they want portrayed and shape the minds of the masses. We are dealing with an ungodly system. Remember, they aren't saved. They won't promote anything that will bring black men into the image of God. If someone tears down blacks by confessing, "They are trifling, they don't want to work, men are no good," the media will support them and help them write books.

PROPHETIC PRINCIPLE #62

Media aids in the dehumanizing of blacks!

They will interview you asking, "Have you been hurt by men?" You will say, "Yes." Their next question will be, "How do you feel about black men?" And you will fall right into the trap by responding, "They are not any good. They're just altogether messed up!" Then they will say, "come, sign the contract right here for us to publish your story." They'll ask someone else, "How do you feel about black men?" They'll say, "They are just no good; they can't get a job, there are no decent black men, a good man is hard to find." They will ask, "Do you have an ability to talk?" They will say,"Yes." Then they'll be given a talk show.

PROPHETIC PRINCIPLE #63

Don't be a sellout!

If you want to be successful in this system, all you have to do is hate black men according to the world's system. I have an understanding of Kingdom principles. The devil only shows up at the doors of miracles. He only shows up at the doors of champions. He only shows up because he fears what is in your future. We have a glorious future and that is why the enemy has showed up at the door of my people. There is a glorious future if you hear the Word of the Lord!

CURRENT-DAY SOCIETAL ILLS

We must begin to understand the ills of today. Integration did not help blacks as a people. Since integration, our poor have become poorer. Integration was a way of saying, "Blacks, y'all come over here to be educated by us whites so that we can rid you of your identity and uniqueness." They will interpret what you are, what you can be, and what you will be. You will be told that you will make a good athlete; you should do something with your hands, like become a mechanic. You've got good balance, why don't you become a sanitation engineer...

PROPHETIC PRINCIPLE #64

Integration was NOT the mind of God!

Integration was not in the mind of our oppressor when he was espousing civil rights. And if the Church doesn't deal with the issue, then who has the authority to address it and bring resolution? The Church is supposed to be the institution that speaks for the concept and Person of Truth, to correct the wrong and make it right. The Church is called to expose that which is unrighteous, destroy it, and bring forth that which is righteous.

We must bring justice into a system that is unrighteous. What we have had was not really integration, but cultural surrender. You are judged as guilty if you begin to pick up your culture. We have been taught that God can't use your culture. Not only are you in a system that attempts to destroy our culture, but they try to make everything about your culture - Africans - appear negative.

When you look at the picture of the Last Supper, Judas has the most darkened skin color. When it is a bad lie, it's a black lie, but when it's not so bad it's "a white lie." When you go to the bakery and ask for angel food cake, the cake is white. But if you ask for devil's food, they give you cake that looks black.

When you are guilty of betraying someone they don't call it "whitemail," but "blackmail." We live in a society that makes everything that is black look evil or corrupt, and everything that is white look light and all right.

PROPHETIC PRINCIPLE #65

Black is not evil, but beautiful!

We are dealing with a corrupt society; an evil society that has dehumanized a race of people. We need to stop embracing the subliminal messages that they are sending us that white equals right, and understand that some things that are white (pills, salt, sugar, flour) can also be evil.

When you are dealing with people who have a slave mentality, they always want to reach back into slavery for the food that they had in Egypt. You are killing yourself with the salt, sugar, and flour — let go of the three white killers!

Someone may ask, "Are you against white people?" No, that would be total stupidity. But we are against white supremacy - white male dominance - that has come to enslave or to make you and I look inferior. Even as you begin to climb the corporate ladder, they will show you the American dream, but as you start your ascent, you'll experience the Great American Nightmare as you smash against the invisible glass ceiling. They'll let you see the dream, but they will try to stop your entrance.

Some of you have been bumping your head up against that ceiling lately, and you are trying to figure out what is wrong. You haven't gotten the revelation that you are trying to become something that you are not, so, you are still seeing it, but not getting it.

You are in a system that is designed for you not to make it. When a black man is driving down the street in a BMW vehicle or Mercedes Benz, he gets pulled over by policemen for no other reason than the fact that he's driving an expensive car. He asks, "What did I do officer?" The officer says, "Just shut up, give me your license and registration, and by the way open up your trunk."

You can't be prosperous or look successful as a black man or woman without, in the sight of your oppressor, being viewed as if you have done something illegal. Why is that view there? Because they have created a system where you are not supposed to succeed.

There are certain things that you aren't supposed to have.

PROPHETIC PRINCIPLE #66

Your oppressor despises your success!

Some of you understand what it took just to go to school and get your little piece of paper. You attempted to further your education and they said, "No, you don't need to do that, go around this way." Then you found that you took several courses which were not necessary for your degree. It seems as if there are numerous road blocks that are in your way because you are in a system that was designed for you to fail. But God made you a winner, anyhow!!

You will get in trouble today if you try to walk in the image of God. What is my crime, Officer? You tried to walk in the image of God. What did I do wrong? "Number one, you know who you are. Number two, you are determining your own destiny. Number three, you are not listening to what we are saying. Number four, you are not respecting us. Number five, you refuse to be a boy. The crime is: you are walking in the image of God!"

PROPHETIC PRINCIPLE #67

Don't ask permission!

You have the nerve to walk with your head up! You have the nerve to determine your own economic destiny! You have the nerve to decide how many children you want to have, without stopping at the door of Planned Parenthood! You have the nerve to open up your own business! You have the nerve to say, "America is too small, I am going global with my product."! What is the crime? You decided to walk in the image and likeness of God!

CONFRONTING RACISM

Racism is thriving in the walls of the Church, and freedom is a stranger within her walls. In 1993, God began to speak to me about addressing racism in the Church. He is beginning to bring about another visitation in the earth. For some reason, God is highlighting the issue of racism in our nation.

PROPHETIC PRINCIPLE #68
Judgment begins in the house of God.

Everyone isn't celebrating the liberation of a people. People say that I sound like a racist. But in the sense of its fullest definition, I can't be a racist because I don't have the power to oppress anyone. I don't have the power to force my views on anyone.

According to Webster's Dictionary, I don't have the ability to be a racist. It is not possible. It is interesting, however, that when you start to talk about black issues, it is interpreted in the minds of Americans that you are against whites. I am accused of being guilty for loving myself and my people.

When God brings this next revival, (and we are beginning to feel the first twinges of it), He is coming once again with the same Spirit and power as in times past. The Azusa Street Pentecostal revival really began with a black man, but the Church split over racism. Whites pulled out because they could not see themselves under black leadership. And if you were to believe most accounts that have been written concerning Azusa, you would find that most writers desire to credit white men for the Azusa revival.

It is a real challenge for a white man to submit to the leadership of a black man. He has to deal with 300 years of programming that has been passed down from his ancestors. This programming has told him that blacks are inferior and to submit to black leadership, that would make you inferior as well.

PROPHETIC PRINCIPLE #69

Black leadership threatens the white man!

Because they have dehumanized the black man, many will not receive the deliverance that is needed through black vessels which God will raise up, because of the packaging.

God will probably have a black man discover the cure of AIDS. But, someone will try to strategize a way to believe that they received the solution first. Or, if you come up with a cure, they will try to make it seem as if your cure is not working. They will add one ingredient (that really didn't do anything) and say, "No, yours is not the cure, mine is."

SUFFERING WITH THE OPPRESSED

And I, brethren, when I came to you, came not with excellency of speech or of wisdom, declaring unto you the testimony of God.

For I determined not to know anything among you, save Jesus Christ, and him crucified.

And I was with you in weakness, and in fear, and in much trembling.

I Corinthians 2:1-3

PROPHETIC PRINCIPLE #70

God is raising up Black Deliverers!

Paul didn't speak unto them using a lot of big words. He came in simplicity. There is something about the gospel that can reach everybody.

Paul, who had Roman citizenship, belonged to a nation that was under the oppressor. He threw Christians in jail. But, when he was born again, he identified with the suffering — that is the cross. The cross of the Lord Jesus Christ is not getting born again at the house of the oppressors and remaining among the oppressors in their false doctrine. But the new birth is to be born again, find the Spirit of God among an oppressed people, and pick up the cross of oppression and follow Him.

Moses left the camp of the oppressor, choosing rather to suffer affliction with the people of God than to enjoy the pleasures of sin for a season. Paul left the camp of the oppressor and identified with the struggles of the Church. You can't enjoy the benefits of corporate America and come and speak our language. You must identify totally with the cross of the oppressed — that is the cross.

PROPHETIC PRINCIPLE #71

Leave the camp of your oppressor!

Change won't come in the white community until we see whites leaving out of their churches saying, "We have been called to identify with the oppressed people. We have not come to parent you and tell you how to do it because if we tell you, we can only tell you how to be the oppressor. Rather, we have come to learn from your oppression, we have come to identify with your suffering, and we are asking you to teach us."

The whites who joined with Martin Luther King, Jr in his day didn't salute him as their leader. They joined him to help — they wanted to help teach him and not to be parented by him. The Apostle Paul said:

And I was with you in weakness, and in fear, and in much trembling.

And my speech and my preaching was not with enticing words of man's wisdom, but in demonstration of the Spirit and of power.

That your faith should not stand in the wisdom of men, but in the power of God.

I Corinthians 2:3-5

PROPHETIC PRINCIPLE #72

Whites must see us as leaders and not parent us as children!

In this hour you will have many men who will stand in the wisdom of men. But God is not moving through the wisdom of men nor through great orators. That day is over. In this hour, there will be men who will stand in the power of God, even though they may be splitting their verbs because they are not well versed in English. The men that God is raising up to be deliverers are those who can't necessarily speak fluently, but they will display the power of God. They will begin to operate in the image in which God has created them.

PROPHETIC PRINCIPLE #73

God will use rejects to display His power!

CHAPTER FIVE

UNDERSTANDING THE VOICE OF GOD

When God said, "Let there be," He proceeded to create. The creative word of God is powerful!

When God says something, He is going to bring it to pass. God has already said and declared that He is raising up a people. He has already spoken to us concerning our destiny, our purpose, we have a contribution to bring to the nation. God is calling us in this hour to make that contribution. But before we can, we must be re-identified.

PROPHETIC PRINCIPLE #74

Cultural Identity is important to God!

The children of Israel had to be re-identified when they left the slavery of Egypt. When you have been programmed incorrectly, then you have to be reprogrammed. Some of you need a new identity. Some of you have been identified by your oppressor; programmed into what you must become, assimilating until you have lost your cultural identity.

You went to school and became educated, you took a trip to Europe and travelled to England. There is nothing wrong with visiting those places, but look at the goals that we begin to set as a result of it. It is very rare to will find someone who says, "I went to Africa." If you ask, "Have you ever gone to Africa," they will say, "No, I don't want to go there." In their mind, there has been such a programming against the "Dark Continent" that if you were to tell some people, "You are from Africa," they will say, "I am from Louisiana or Mississippi. Don't tell me that I am from Africa."

You can't interpret your history nor the Scriptures from the perspective of your oppressor. Because our oppressors have been in control, we have to re-educate ourselves concerning the meaning of English words. We have to get to the root of what "love" really means, what "peace" means, and what the "Kingdom" means.

PROPHETIC PRINCIPLE #75

Don't be ashamed of where you originated!

"Kingdom" has been interpreted in the light of a Eurocentric mindset, not in the light of the Scriptures. In the Kingdom that God builds, He tells His disciples that prostitutes will come into it before you will; the despised, and the people that don't have what it takes according to the standards of men.

When you look at Kingdom through the eyes of some scholars, that is not the kingdom that they are talking about. If you, as a black person, begin to preach too much on the Kingdom of God and start addressing social issues, they will say that you are moving away from the gospel. But, the gospel is social; it deals with the whole man and his environment. However, it is not the gospel when a black man preaches it.

The Moral Majority can get up and say, "We represent morality. We hate abortion." No one will say to them, "That gospel's too social." We are preaching the Kingdom of God. They understand that the message of the Kingdom will bring liberation.

When you understand this gospel to the point where the Word of the Lord is in your mouth, and you begin to speak as a prophetic voice, there must be social change. There will be a change in the educational system, if the gospel of the Kingdom really gets into their hands. If the gospel of the Kingdom begins to impact our educational system, we will say, "Stop teaching black history from the inception of slavery, let's go back a little further into our cultural identity."

Since we really want to deal with history, let's take this white Jesus off of the wall and let's get a Jesus up there who has bronze feet and whose hair is wooly and nappy, so that Junior can understand that Jesus looked just like him! Take down that picture over there of Moses, too, cause he didn't have blonde hair and blue eyes, either!

PROPHETIC PRINCIPLE #76

The Word of the Lord will produce social change!

You will ask the teachers, "Why don't those whom we call Jews now look like the Jews who lived then?" Let them ask the teachers those questions so that they can give them some answers. Jesus grew up in Egypt and they look different from what the picture is depicting. Lets take that picture down of the man whom they depict as helping to carry the cross of Jesus and tell them that there was a black man who helped Jesus carry the cross.

Europe really didn't come into the gospel until about 300 AD. When they came into the gospel, they brought a lot of paganism and idolatry with them that polluted the gospel. The images were all changed and shortly thereafter, the Church went into the dark ages because they put the light out in the Church.

PROPHETIC PRINCIPLE #77

The gospel has been polluted by Europeans!

CRUSHING PREPARES YOU FOR PROMOTION

God is coming to bring light again. He is raising up some black men, a despised people who speak in tongues to lay hands on people. He is trying to get His light back into the earth. God is raising up deliverers. He is having ravens feed you; preachers whose packages you don't particularly care for.

There is an anointing that comes when you have been through mess. Eventually your manure will catch ahold of a seed. We have mixed this unadulterated word into the life that has been through some mess, the manure begins to embrace it and out of it comes life. The olive does not become precious until it has been crushed. There is something about the oil that God is bringing out of the lives of messengers in this hour. But, in order for the oil in their lives to impact this generation, they have to experience the crushing.

PROPHETIC PRINCIPLE #78

If you have been walked on you are a candidate for the anointing!

Grapes become valuable when they are crushed. In the old days when they made wine, someone had to get down there and walk on the grapes. People have repeatedly told you, "You are nothing, you will never be anything, and you are no good." Some of you have been through situations where you were not promoted. They say, "You are no good, you are not going anywhere, I am going to keep you down." They didn't understand that they were preparing the wine.

Don't complain about the crushing; don't run from the crushing, don't try to escape the crushing because God is preparing the wine that is about to be served. You are just being prepared.

Something is happening in this hour and some people are getting disturbed because they are saying, "We thought we crushed them." Somehow, they are still influencing the nation. To our critics; you won't be able to put out what God has started! God is doing some unusual things. He is raising up some unusual people. He is raising up people who were not supposed to have anything to say.

PROPHETIC PRINCIPLE #79

God is breaking the silence over His people!

For he spake, and it was done; he commanded, and it stood fast.

Psalm 33:9

The counsel of the Lord standeth for ever, the thoughts of his heart to all generations.

Psalm 33:11

When God speaks, it is done. When He commands, it stands fast. God is speaking and He is telling the Church, "Let us make man." "How do you want man made?" "In My image, after My likeness."

PICKING UP THE CROSS OF JESUS

What is picking up the cross of Jesus in this hour? Picking up the cross of Jesus means to pick up the struggle for oppressed people; that is the cross. You won't get stoned for your confession of faith. Your life won't get threatened because you confess that you are healed.

PROPHETIC PRINCIPLE #80

Don't be afraid to pick up the cross!

If you lobby in Washington and say, "There needs to be reparation." They will say, "What are you talking about?" Our answer would be, "We are here to get the check for African-American people who have been devastated through slavery. We don't want the mule now, we want the Mercedes. The mule has interest tagged on it, and besides, mules are sterile. God's about multiplication!! We don't want the 40 acres now. We need acres and structures on the acres, which house entire cities."

Why? To begin to pay them for their losses and to bring them up to the level that they are supposed to be in society — that is repentance. There is no repentance unless there is a check in your hands. Don't apologize and say, "I am sorry for what my ancestors did. We really didn't have anything to do with it." Well, you are benefiting from it, so what do you mean that you didn't have anything to do with it? That is stupidity.

PROPHETIC PRINCIPLE #81

Your oppressor owes you!

Someone told me on a talk show that they didn't have anything to do with the past injustices. They don't understand that they are benefiting from the situation. That is why they own the type of property that they have. There is not a black-owned hotel in New York City. I still don't think that we own a ball team.

We don't own any stadiums. We don't own any networks, yet we love television and athletics. We make these institutions wealthy by supporting them.

God has brought a people to this nation, a people who have been despised, a people that He has elected to convict a society of the injustices that have been done. He is saying, "Now, it is time for the gospel to come forth and to go into the hearts of men in order to bring change." You had better believe that when God speaks, things change. Everything and everyone complies to the Voice of God!

PROPHETIC PRINCIPLE #82

Now is the time for change!

CHAPTER SIX
DIVINE ELECTION

For ye see your calling, brethren, how that not many wise men after the flesh, not many mighty, not many noble, are called.

I Corinthians 1:26

In other words, God is not calling many individuals out of the halls of academia. God has chosen the foolish things of the world to confound the wise. He will use and anoint people who were not supposed to make it. To the individual that is not supposed to be exalted, God is saying, "I am raising you up without anyone's permission. I am not through with you."

"...God hath chosen the weak things of the world to confound the things which are mighty.

And the base things of the world, and things which are despised, hath God chosen, yea, and things which are not, to bring to nought things that are."

I Corinthians 1:27-28

PROPHETIC PRINCIPLE #83
God chooses the un-elected!

In this hour, God is using weak things. He is throwing mice at the elephant's feet and the elephant is going to dance! He is using a people who are disenfranchised, have no economics, eating food that others would not eat, living where others would not live; homeless and landless.

Blacks were despised for a purpose. However the 1960's protestors never completed the task that they were supposed to in that generation, so God allowed us to skip around that block. We sang, "Free at last, free at last, thank God Almighty I'm free at last," but we never really entered into true liberation.

We thought we were free. We just had a few chains removed, but we're still running around in circles because we are not controlling the ship. In the 1990's, a generation later, we find that our forefathers did not complete their assignment. Now God, through His mighty Hand, is removing the oppression.

PROPHETIC PRINCIPLE #84

Break free from the mental chains!

When the prophets were speaking and singing their songs a generation ago, that music had a message in it. They were trying to tell us something. They saw a Kingdom that we didn't quite understand. God is now bringing us around the corner and saying, "I am bringing you into something that your prophets were trying to tell you, but you couldn't hear them because of the packaging." We are talking about a liberation that is going to come through the power of the gospel of Jesus Christ.

God chose those things that are despised. He didn't choose the accepted thing. If you are accepted, then you don't qualify. But, if you are a reject, then you qualify! When Europeans come to my church and say, "I want to be a member and I am submitting to you as my pastor," they have just enrolled in the school of rejection. Some of their great grandmothers are turning over in their graves.

God calls rejects. The greater the rejection, the greater the anointing. "....And the things which are not...." In the minds of some people, you don't even exist. They have their plans for you in the year 2000. You are not even on the agenda. "We are going to take jobs from America into Mexico and other places so we don't even need your little field hands anymore."

PROPHETIC PRINCIPLE #85

God uses despised things!

We have been in a system that has taught us to be workers. Even though you may own your own business, you are still a slave until you become a producer. The one who sells the product is still not independently wealthy. It is not until you become a producer of a product that you really enter into wealth because you set the price of the product. In other words, you must go somewhere as a people and create a car out of Africa that can compete with the current market; a look that is not already on the market. We must become the manufacturers.

PROPHETIC PRINCIPLE #86

Become a producer - not a seller!

We have been in a system where we have made everyone else wealthy, yet we remain poor. This is why I say, "Blacks who are worshipping in white churches have no business worshipping there until their own community becomes economically empowered." How can you go and rejoice in another land when your own land is not free? When your financial strength leaves the community, then it leaves the rest of the community to bear in a struggle for freedom and liberation alone. You go elsewhere to worship, then when liberation comes you will come back and rejoice with us and say, "We did it." No, you went to the other side during the times of struggle and never helped in the development of your own Jerusalem.

If all African-Americans, who are worshipping under white leadership, came out and worshipped in black churches, can you imagine what kind of staff can begin to be developed? If they brought the kind of tithes and offerings that they were giving in those institutions, they can develop their own community and create jobs right in the local assembly. Some of your local black ministers who are struggling to carry the gospel would not be working a secular 9 to 5 job and picking up a second job to keep the church lights on. Then you say, "He just doesn't preach the Word." Well, you are not giving. You are not providing the help and strength that he needs to bear the load.

PROPHETIC PRINCIPLE #87

Minister to your Jerusalem FIRST!

We need to understand who God is choosing. He is choosing the despised. "...the things which are not, to bring to nought the things that are...." God is setting you up and you don't even know it.

God is restoring man in this hour. God said, "Let us make man in our image, after our likeness and let them have dominion." You were not created to be ruled over, but to rule, to have dominion. You were not created to be a slave because that is not the image of God. Neither were you created to be inferior; that is not the image of God.

God says in His Word, "Let us make man." The law of dominion states: "Whatever I don't have dominion over, will have dominion over me".

God is raising up a new and radical generation.

THE PROMISE TO GENERATIONS

Now the Lord had said unto Abram, Get thee out of thy country, and from thy kindred, and from thy father'shouse, unto a land that I will show thee: And I will make of thee a great nation, and I will bless thee, and make thy name great; and thou shalt be a blessing:

And I will bless them that bless thee, and curse him that curseth thee: and in thee shall all families of the earth be blessed.

So Abram departed, as the Lord had spoken unto him; and Lot went with him: and Abram was seventy and five years old when he departed out of Haran.

Genesis 12:1-4

PROPHETIC PRINCIPLE #88

Your seed is covered through the blessings of Abraham.

God is dealing with Abram. When God begins to make covenant with a man, He is not only talking to that man, but He is speaking to his nation.

When you come into covenant with God, He is going to make your name great. He is going to throw your name up in lights. Your name can't be made great without wealth. It costs money to get the neon lights up!

As a people, we didn't have a vision beyond the front of the bus. We almost should have stayed in the back of the bus because as long as we were, we were in the struggle; we always had a vision of the front of the bus. It wasn't until we came into the front of the bus that we became settled with having a front seat.

But we still don't have anything. We should own a bus by now. We should have envisioned manufacturing the buses. We must become producers. The image of God is to produce.

PROPHETIC PRINCIPLE #89

Maintain a vision of progression!

When you touch a man of God, you bring a curse in your life. Be very watchful of the voices that you touch in this hour. If you curse God's anointed, He will curse you!

According to Genesis chapter one, when God speaks it happens. If it doesn't happen in your generation, it will happen in the next. God told the children of Israel that He was taking them to a land that He would show them. That generation didn't enter into the promised land, but that doesn't mean God lied. When He speaks, He also speaks to your seed and your seed's seed. So, if you are not ready to enter in, then He will wait for you to die, and your children will enter into the promise.

I believe that we may have been going around in the wilderness; we have walked around in a circle. We had to wait until some old mindsets died out. We had some mindsets that kept wanting to go back to Egypt; "Lets go back to the good old days, where at least we could eat onions, garlic, and leeks. We were bending and stooping, but at least we were eating." God is letting us know that there are some people who have to die out in the desert because the next generation is saying, "We are not going back."

PROPHETIC PRINCIPLE #90

God moves from generation to generation.

Even in church we were singing, "Let us all go back to the old landmark." I don't want to go back, I want to press forward!

God made a promise to Abram. He told him that He was going to make him a father of many nations. God talked to a man without a seed. Abram was a man who didn't have a future. The only future that he had was the word of the Lord. Sarah was past the years of child-bearing. When the promise was given, she laughed because she knew that she had experienced menopause. Abram was impotent.

God knows how to take an impotent man and a woman who was past menopause and work in that situation. When God speaks something, He will do whatever He needs to problems your body might present.

PROPHETIC PRINCIPLE #91

Never underestimate the power of God!

GOD QUICKENS
THAT WHICH IS DEAD

(As it is written, I have made thee a father of many nations,) before him whom he believed, even God, who quickeneth the dead, and calleth those things which be not as though they were.

Romans 4:17

When God elects you for a function, even though men have declared that it is dead, He gets in it and quickens it. He brings it to life.

PROPHETIC PRINCIPLE #92

God breathes life into those things that are dead!

When the Word of the Lord came, Sarah began feeling young again. Abraham started looking because it was time for the promise. When it is time for your prophecy concerning marriage to be fulfilled, you start looking. There is an attitude that changes. You take a posture that says, "I am about to walk into my blessing. I feel it coming. Where? I don't know, but God is quickening something that is dead." When your Boaz is on the way, you start fixing yourself up and you don't even know why! You are getting yourself together because you know that your prophecy is beginning to come to pass!

I hold this philosophy: you should dress for where you are going and not for where you have been. Some of you are trying to attract a number 10 man, but you are still living at the level of number one. You have to fix yourself up. When you fix yourself up and become a 10, then a ten will come to you. You may be saying, "I don't know why I keep getting proposals from "ones" and "twos." Sister, look in the mirror!

PROPHETIC PRINCIPLE #93

You only attract what you see yourself as!

God calleth those things that be not as though they were.

> *Who against hope believed in hope, that he might become the father of many nations, according to that which was spoken, So shall thy seed be.*

Romans 4:17,18

The Word of the Lord has gone forth that this is the hour of the black man. God is going to cause the black man to emerge. He is causing a people who have been oppressed to come forth. This is why we are seeing the shake-ups in South Africa. This is why we are seeing a new generation coming forth. They say, "I don't want church the way it used to be — that kind of church is crippling. We need a church that will declare unto us the truth."

God is quickening that which is dead in this hour because the word has already been spoken. Abram had unwavering faith. Verse 19, "And being not weak in faith, he considered not his own body now dead, when he was about an hundred years old, neither yet the deadness of Sarah's womb."

Stop considering your feelings. You will go crazy if you look at the news today! Stop considering your environment! Stop considering the situation! You have to keep your eyes focused on the promise!

The Bible says when Abraham was about 100 years old, he considered not his own body, neither yet the deadness of Sarah's womb. He wouldn't even consider it.

"He staggered not at the promises of God through unbelief; but was strong in faith, giving glory to God"

Romans 4:20

PROPHETIC PRINCIPLE #94

Believe only in the promises of God!

There is something in blacks that is radical. We are radical by nature. There is something about our dance that is radical. There is something about our speech that is radical. There is something about our faith in God that becomes radical. We have a way of swimming upstream against the odds. We change everything with which we come in contact.

You are just like the children of Israel of old, who were black skinned people — when you show up, you drive them out! Move into their neighborhoods and see if you won't see the "for sale" signs going up! Go into an all white swimming pool, take your children and jump in the water; you will clear the pool! You change everything!

PROPHETIC PRINCIPLE #95

The oppressor is intimidated by our very presence.

When you show up in certain places of the corporate ladder, they change the rules of the game. We are inventors by nature. When we were running numbers in the community up in Harlem, and were making a profit they took that and marketed it and set up OTB!

And being fully persuaded, that what he had promised, he was able also to perform.

Romans 4:21

You need to keep looking at the promises of God. There are some people who are saying that it is over for you. They are saying that your day is over; your lights are out; you will never become anything. But, you must stop looking at the struggle, stop "considering" what you are up against and stagger not at the promise. For the promises of God unto you are "Yea"; He's simply waiting for you to utter the "AMEN!!!"

PROPHETIC PRINCIPLE #96

It's time to walk out the promises of God!

VIDEO CASSETTES
BY BISHOP E. BERNARD JORDAN

RACIAL ETHICS OF THE KINGDOM

Confronts the intrinsic racism that has permeated Christian doctrine. A Thorough study of the "traditional" teachings of the Church unveils a deliberate strain of racism that fosters white supremacy and eradicates the image of God within the African-American. It was this same strain of religiosity that soothed the consciousness of many and justified the atrocities of slavery in America. This series delineates the patent effects of such doctrine and restores the dignity of all races under God that were created for His divine purpose. 4-Video series $80

FREEDOM: THE WAY OF LIBERATION

A clarification of God's true definition of freedom and the resulting implications of the facade of liberty that continues to enslave the African-American community. The continuous assault of malevolent imagery that society uses to deliberately cripple the function of an entire race of people and deface their cultural legacy actually recreates Jesus Christ, the anointed Deliver of men, into an effigy that is crucified afresh on a daily basis. True freedom will emerge as the traditions of men are dethroned and replaced by the uncompromising Word of God that will cut every insidious lie asunder. This series will offend many who have been blinded by the hypnotic lies that have lulled their purpose to sleep, and challenge others to look beyond the veil of mediocrity and prejudice and behold the beauty of God's original intention towards men. This four-tape series is an unforgettable encounter with past, present and future as it proclaims the manifest destiny of the African-American and the Kingdom of God. 4-Video series $80

A PASSAGE TO LIBERATION

"A Passage to Liberation" is a thought-provoking edict against the dichotomy of society's offer of "Liberation" towards the African-American, versus their true liberty as ordained by God. The ingrained levels of prejudice that are encountered on a daily basis are indicated through the ethical teachings of the Word of God. Your spirit will be stirred to defy the implied boundaries of racial denigration, and thrust into the zenith of your capabilities through Jesus Christ. 4-Video series $80

PREPARATION FOR LEADERSHIP

A scathing indictment upon the insidious racism that permeates American society. Using Exodus Chapter 2 as his premise, Bishop Jordan delivers a powerful comparison between the pattern of oppressive leadership that requires divine intervention in the affairs of men and culminated in the appointment of Moses as the deliverer of Israel with the oppressive leadership that the African-American encounters within society and within the walls of the Church. Frightening in its accuracy, this teaching, though disturbing to the ear, is truly the Word of the Lord for this hour, for there are serious ramifications that the Church must contend with if she is to bring a solution to the crisis of woe in this nation. 4-Video series $80

THE SPIRIT OF THE OPPRESSOR

This series, The Spirit of the Oppressor, by Bishop E. Bernard Jordan, attacks the very fiber of societal influence that manipulates the gospel to justify racial supremacy. The insidious attitudes that permeate the Church are also addressed, for judgment begins in the House of God. By understanding that the Church is called to be the example for the world to follow, this series is powerful in its ability to expose the evil that lurks in the shadows of the "acceptable norm," and echoes a clarion call for deliverance from the lie that masquerades as the truth. Are you REALLY ready for the Word of the Lord?

4-Video series .... $80 also available as a book.

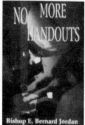

NO MORE HANDOUTS

In this series, Bishop E. Bernard Jordan addresses an inflammatory issue that has been instilled as a mindset within an entire nation of people. The American society has methodically caused generations of African-Americans to become dependent to a system that keeps them in a cycle of expectation that the government will always be their source of blessing. Bishop Jordan delineates the intention of God to bring prosperity to His people, thus charging them to turn their attention from the governmental system and discover the treasure that God has placed in their hands, for God is to be their source! This series is challenging and will force you to use your God-given abilities to thing creatively and generate wealth. You don't need anyone's permission to increase, for God has already decreed that you would multiply and wax exceedingly mighty!! This radical message is for a radical people!!

4-Video series $80

THE CROSSING

Bishop E. Bernard Jordan delivers a powerful teaching that defines the attitude that one must take as they begin to cross over their Jordan into the promised land. The paradigms of the old must be shattered as the image of change comes into view. One cannot embrace a new day loaded with old apparatus that is inoperative; old concepts that only brought you to a place of desperation and frustration. Rather, one must search the Word of God and renew your mind to Kingdom thinking that will bring elevation into your life. This series will sweep the cobwebs of mediocrity out of your life, and provoke you to a higher plane of right thinking that will thrust you into the path of dreams fulfilled. Straightforward in his approach, Bishop Jordan preaches a message that is inflammatory to the lies that have taken residence in your mind, and instills the purity of truth that is the nature of Almighty God. 4-Video series $80

UNDRESSING THE LIE

In this series, Bishop E. Bernard Jordan addresses a crucial issue in the Body of Christ -- RACISM. This series will captivate those who are true lovers of truth, for Jesus Christ is the Truth, and many have hidden Him and His cultural reality from the eyes of many. By conducting a thorough search of the Scriptures, Bishop Jordan identifies the Bible's description of Jesus that has been marred by the lies of those who wished to destroy an entire nation's concept of themselves, instead rendering theology that warped the image of God and denigrated them by teaching that they were cursed. Questions that have wandering in the minds of many for hundreds of years are answered as Bishop Jordan takes a strong stand to unmask the lies that have been masquerading as Truth. 4-Video series $80

LEGACY

In this series, Bishop E. Bernard Jordan expounds upon the African presence within the Scriptures. Combatting the misnomers that Africans were cursed by God and that they had very little to do with the unfolding of Biblical events, Bishop Jordan smashes the veil of delusion to cause the obvious truth to surface. During this season, God is causing a cultural renaissance to emerge. The oppressor of American society has lulled the minds of most people into a stupor of ignorance leaving them landless, powerless, and, once again, easy to enslave. The historical accounts within the Scriptures have been bequeathed as a legacy from our ancestors to proclaim the Word of the Lord against the sophisticated genocide that is affecting the African-American. A nation that ignores its past is doomed to repeat its failures in the future. Bishop Jordan brings clarity and balance to an inflammatory topic that is frequently misunderstood. 4-Video series $80

ECONOMICS: THE PATH TO EMPOWERMENT

This vital tape series by Bishop E. Bernard Jordan and Prophet Robert Brown deals with God's answers to the financial instability that has crippled the strength of the African-American nation. By defining the true motivation behind the onslaught of racism, Bishop Jordan and Prophet Brown give clear answers to the persistent societal obstacles that prevent most people from obtaining the true manifestation of God's intention for prosperity in their lives. The articulate questions that proceed from the heart of the nation shall be answered through the accumulation of wealth, for money shall answer all things. This teaching will expose the subtle racism that affects your financial future, and will provoke you into a mindset that will see obstacles as opportunities so that the full potential of God within you may express in your success!
2-Video series $40

NO LIBERATION WITHOUT VIOLENCE

This series will cause one to Scripturally discern the validity of the message of liberation that echoed through America during the 60's through Dr. Martin Luther King and Malcolm X. By holding their messages up to the scrutiny of the Word of God, one cannot help but conclude whose message was more palatable to society, versus the message that stood in the integrity of the Scripture. Challenging in its content, this series is designed to attack the shackles of passivity and charge you to recognize the brutal realities of today's society. You are called to understand the true liberty of the gospel that Jesus preached. 4-Video series $80

A NEW GENERATION

Bishop E. Bernard Jordan is at his best in this series which portrays the change in one's attitude that must take place in order to attain your maximum potential in God and proceed to your Canaan Land! Like Joshua, one must be ready to be strong and of a good courage as you confront racism in this day. This is a radical message to eradicate error and bring forth the truth! Cutting in its intensity, this series will show you how the Word of the Lord will render you untouchable when you are aware of your purpose!! Bishop Jordan defines the new breed of people that God is raising up that will know the art of war, understand and love their enemy as they embrace the arms of destiny fulfilled.
4-Video series $80

ORDER FORM

ZOE MINISTRIES

4702 FARRAGUT ROAD • BROOKLYN, NY 11203 • (718) 282-2014

TITLE	QTY	DONATION	TOTAL

Guarantee: You may return any defective item within 90 days for replacement. All offers are subject to change without notice. Please allow 4 weeks for delivery. No COD orders accepted. Make checks payable to ZOE MINISTRIES.

Subtotal	
Shipping	
Donation	
TOTAL	

Name: _____Phone _____

Address: _____

_____Zip _____

Payment by: Check or Money Order (Payable to Zoe Ministries)
Visa • MasterCard • American Express • Discover

Card No.: _____ Exp. Date)_____

Signature (Required) _____